*I thank God Almighty.
The giver of gifts.*

*I thank Payal and Angad,
they are a blessing.*

QUOTES
BY
PARAMJIT SINGH

MIND & HEART

1. Being mindful of your own mind should be an everyday activity.

2. It's your mind that makes you do stupid, mediocre or great things.

3. A compassionate thought means nothing if you don't put it in action.

4. The right intent of the heart decorates an action.

5. We should be very aware of our own intentions.

6. The motive is more important than the act.

7. Wish others well and be well yourself.

8. Let your heart be filled with an abundance of goodness, wellness and happiness.

9. Being wrongly opinionated is worse than being ignorant.

10. To know yourself better, spend more time with yourself.

11. The best words come to us in silences.

12. Silence is a state full of dynamic energy.

13. Be truthful to yourself and you will not be fooled.

14. If you can sit with someone in comfortable silence, you are in the company of a friend.

MIND & HEART

16. Miracles are all around us. It's in the flower in front of you.

17. When the wise speak, listen to the words and the silence.

18. Inquiry of self is an essential activity.

19. The fool is for ever giving advice. Fervently honing his foolishness skills.

20. People who come into power without earning or working for it are very dangerous.

21. The hardship that you endured today will become your strength tomorrow.

22. Contentious people are assassins of happiness, joy and all things good.

23. Just for one more day, each day, don't give up and you will succeed.

24. Intelligence makes things simple.

25. Simple is always profound.

26. Learn, unlearn, learn. That's how you grow.

27. Movement is the law of the universe.

28. To know the deeper meaning of things, man's soul has to be at times - Still.

29. To the one afraid, the movement of the curtain is always suspicious.

30. The measure of a man is known once he opens his mouth.

31. The measure of a man is known in his treatment of people less fortunate than him.

32. Let love burn bright.

DRIVE

1.

I was watching a bird fly from my balcony, flapping its wings hard to go forward against a strong contrary wind. Suddenly the wind changed and its struggle ceased. With open wings, she floated effortlessly towards her destination.
The wind is about to change.
Spread your wings.

2.   It is a new day. With new hope. Rise shine sparkle.

3.   A small seed has tree in it. For it to fulfill its destiny, it has to get planted. Stay planted and bear much fruit. Once in a while Fly.

4.   When you traverse, both, the valleys and the mountains, you will understand that both are needed. In fact, they complement each other.

5.   What excites you, becomes your direction. So, what excites you?

6.   If life was always a bed of roses, half a thorn would kill you.

DRIVE

7. Everything has been said before, but not like you will say it.

8. A song in your heart preserves the spring in your step.

9. Don't lose the fight in your head. The rest of you will catch up.

10. People with wisdom are reluctant teachers. They understand responsibility.

11. Give of yourself to others and increase.

12. Avoid people who carry their greatness on their sleeve.

13. A great sportsman can dig deep into the reservoir of his soul and stand up again.

LIFE

1. Appreciation enhances Life.

2. When your neighbor's prosperity gladdens your heart, you have truly arrived.

3. One of the joys of life is looking at old pictures of your children.

4. A grudge will kill you, not the other guy.

5. Many times in life, someone else's composure, composes you.

6.
If you know the truth with certainty, the urge to prove your point will go away.

7. Anything which is said repeatedly tends to lose its meaning, especially with children.

8. Let the opinion of others educate you, but never control you.

9. Seasons change… love does not, it remains.

10. My son surprises me with his insight, quite pleasantly, many a times.
Listen to the young.

TRUTH IN JEST

1.

Wit is a stpontaneous utterance of what you truthfully, and without bias, have observed in the last hour or a lifetime.

2.

Wit is a sibling of truth.

3.

Plants and books are great decoration for a home.

4.

Keep the Swag. Ditch the brag.

5. The eyes of a man cannot hide what he wishes to conceal.

6. People have so many negative things to say about cellphones, and then you see them standing in a long queue to get the latest one.

7. A serious ailment is going around these days. It is known as constipation of the mind. Hardly anything goes in and nothing comes out, and what is inside, is decaying.

8. It takes a toll on the pompous to survive the regimen of pomposity.

THE WAY OF WISDOM

1.

One has to grow up… and still be a child. Wonderful it is!

2.

True humility brings easy confidence. Pride brings in misery.

3.

Teaching someone what you know will ensure, that you will never forget what you taught. Each one teach one. Share what you know; it will make you happier.

4. Following people with no vision is the fastest way to get to nowhere.

5. My daughter's laughter never fails to put a smile on my face.

6. Adversity can lead to prosperity, ignorance to knowledge, weakness to strength and sorrow to joy…if one is willing to learn.

7. I will always look for virtue and good in a man, without my past experiences coloring my view. I firmly believe, in most cases, what you seek you shall find.

8. Time flies by, but memories remain. I wish you happy and victorious ones. Memories that give you hope of a better tomorrow.

9. I love human beings. This has its ups and downs, but I continue to love.

10. The child in me is ever ready to do a cartwheel.

THE WAY OF WISDOM

11. Some of the nicest people I've met were ordinary.

12. Don't waste food. Take it with you and you will find someone who is hungry. Give it to him.

13. I am not ambitious, I just love what I do.

14. Don't carry your past on your shoulders. Learn from it and move on.

15. The past is generally exalted, the future is mostly uncertain and pessimistic but the present is generally ridiculed. Why is that?

16. Speak the Truth to yourself. That is more than half the job done.

17. Laughter balances exasperation.

18. Thought has a source, keep it good.

19. Most people like a post which says, money is coming your way. No harm, but I would much rather have wisdom coming my way.

20. Sow smiles, reap laughter.

21. Let us for a time, hear more and speak less.

22. One moment of truth, can give you a direction for a lifetime.

23. Compassion keeps you young. Try it.

24. Self-righteousness is a disease.

THE WAY OF WISDOM

25. We have so many opinions about others. Do we have the correct one for ourselves?

26. Sometimes, the last thing people see is the obvious.

27. Sometimes questions are wiser than answers.

28. Energy cannot be destroyed. Sound is energy. What you speak cannot be undone. Think before you speak.

29. Truth is a safe destination. Enjoy the journey.

30. Money does not make people. People make money. Respect people… use money for good.

31. I am amazed at the fact that people pay big amounts of money in a fancy restaurant, without complaining, and on their way back, negotiate and argue with a balloon seller at a Mumbai traffic signal to reduce his price from five rupees to three. Something is wrong somewhere.

32. The greatest bond between man and animal is trust. The same happens to be amongst men.

33. Most people think they know better but keep getting worse.

34. A mind clouded with lofty ideas about oneself is like a block of cement. Nothing comes out and nothing goes in. A prison it is.

35. Don't take yourself too seriously. You are still very capable of slipping on a banana peel.

TRUTH, COURAGE & WINGS

1. When you sincerely look for the truth, it finds you.

2. In the long run, humility always turns out stronger than arrogance.

3. There is nothing too hard for God, so don't be too hard on yourself.

4. Truth has no value for a self-righteous person.

5. Love doesn't need a reward. It needs a response.

6. Money is a by product of loving the work that you do. It is incidental, as it should be.

7. Don't just call people when you have a problem…call them also when you rejoice.

8. Courage will arrive when you start doing what you fear.

9. He was all icing but no cake.

10. Keep your mind on things bigger than yourself.

11. People full of themselves mostly contain nothing of any value.

12. The person was a bull in a china shop, but claimed to love glassware.

13. The day men and women realise that they themselves are imperfect, perfection arrives with its own tools and starts you on a journey of betterment. Enjoy the experience..

14. Some people just want to be unhappy. They mistake it for religiosity.

15. Most people who are trying to change the world, change nothing. The ones who see their own faults and change themselves, many a time, leave a positive change in the people and the world around them.

LOOKING AT LIFE & SOME IRONIES

1. The most silent man in the room oftentimes turns out the wisest.

2. Employers want smart 27-year-olds with 30 years' experience. Not going to happen.

3. Abstract and vague words are the way of the fake intellectual. Don't get confused. He already is.

4. Sometimes, more than clothes, tongues need to be Laundered.

5. Self-righteousness is like soot. If you let it accumulate, it will block all pathways of reason and light.

LOOKING AT LIFE & SOME IRONIES

6.
Self-righteous people are indignant about most things.

7.
I find over-indignation mostly suspect.

8.
Anger never leads to a good place.

9.
Shoving things under the carpet will make the whole house stink.

10.
Deception is an art of thinking that you are right... when you are wrong.

11.
Nobody knows everything…not even you.

13. Freedom with responsibility is everyone's right.

14. The mind of man comes to a standstill when he thinks he knows it all. Then it goes into a little box resembling a coffin, and that's that.

15. Avoid self-pity like the plague.

16. For the mind to start working, the television has to be turned off - Often.

17. Collect good things, go on, discover new ones… pass them on.

18. If you want to achieve greatness without knowing the basics, a crash is on its way. A house is built from floor to ceiling.

THE RHYTHM OF LIFE

1. Time moves at its own pace. Learn it's rhythm and keep up with it.

2. There are people who spread sunshine and good cheer, and there are some who specialize in giving out misery and darkness.
Stick with the former.

3. Truth shows up in unusual ways.

4. The reward of helping someone is in the very act itself.
Don't look elsewhere.

5. When you recognize motives, you recognize people.

6. Of all the languages I don't speak, gibberish is the one I recognize fastest.

7. 'I don't know' is a sentence you should be able to say.

8. Let your mind work in happiness.

9. To learn every day is to live every day.

10. Truth has a hardy spine.

11. Don't doubt anybody's pain.

12. To discern is to be free.

13. The pen is mightier than the sword – After the war.

14. He thought his perpetual expression of disapproval made him stand out in a crowd. He was right.

15. A big part of her demeanor was to make people uneasy.

16. The more they condemn, the more righteous they feel - some people.

17. The wise are not too eager to speak. The fool is a motormouth.

THE RHYTHM
OF LIFE

18. If you know you are right, the urge to argue goes away.

19. People who can laugh at themselves are generally successful.

20. Intelligence is a good thing, but when combined with wisdom, it is marvelous.

21. Pomposity repels wisdom and is a glutton of ignorance.

22. There is always error in pride, and wisdom contains ample humility.

23. Wisdom is not only in what is said, but also in what is left unsaid.

24. Wisdom takes you places where intelligence cannot.

25. Mostly things that are rare are more precious. Get wisdom.

26. Avoid self-righteous people. They are never good company and are repetitive.

AWESOME AROUND US

1. God is not even looking at your righteousness. There isn't Any.
    He is looking for His in you.

2. The knowledge of God is not information, but revelation.

3. An answer is just a prayer away.

4. Two things could happen to you, you may live or die. Both are not
    in your control. Trust the one who controls both.

5. We all have needs. Trust God who has unlimited Resources.

6. One of the most wonderful Words in the language of English is
    Grace. Unmerited favor.

7. On my mind is my Awe of God.

8.
Happiness is above money and success.
Both together it is pure bliss. It only happens,
when God is in it.

9.
Whatever the circumstances, good or bad,
if you are alive and breathing, Thank God.

10.
Have a wonderful day friends and do
expect…Good News.

AWESOME AROUND US

11. If you are going through a bad time now, remember, God makes all things beautiful in His time.

12. To understand love, you have to practice it.

13. Doing your best and leaving the rest to God reduces panic.

14. I did a thousand push-ups and also a cartwheel. I swung around a moon beam and crossed a million seas. The applause was deafening, it was hard to be humble, you see. I turned to take a bow and bumped into someone with pierced hands and feet. Everything faded into oblivion…What remains is Him and me.

15. Only God can deal with a billion people individually and personally, and set them free if they cooperate.

16. Wisdom from above is a Rock you can stand firmly on and not be moved. Worldly wisdom is like straw a in a strong wind.

17. There are things God does, and things that you have to do. Do your part.

18. Sometimes we feel people will destroy us, and then God turns up.

19. The child in me keeps going to God, and he takes me in his arms, always.

20. You may be a 100 years old, but you remain, still and always, a child of God.

AWESOME AROUND US

21. The purpose of a tree is in its seed, but we have to find our purpose - because we have free will.

22. Wisdom will get you much more than money ever will.

23. I am in a thought of God. Awesome. (God thinks about me. Awesome!)

24. She wanted to reach God, but religiosity got in her way.

25. Someone's bad attitude should not change my good one.

26. If you can changes your thoughts, your actions will change too. And so will your world.

27. To learn everyday is one of the greatest privileges given to man. And what you learn, use for good.

28. She could not speak any good for anything or anybody – thinking it would take her away from God.

HAPPINESS

1. Follow your heart, but don't lose your mind.

2. Joy is a very potent tonic. Don't lose it.

3. Don't let anyone or anything steal your joy. It happens to be your strength.

4. Magic is also in the little everyday things that you do with joy.

5. Children make the world go merrily round.

MIGHTIER THAN THE SWORD

1. Nothing can replace writing. It cleanses you.

2. I love the smell of old books, and the worlds within them.

3. No book is complete fiction.

4. Keep a notebook handy. It may invite you to write.

VERSE

1. The trajectory of my thought bounced upon the river waters and headed toward the hills.

   The temperature dropped, and it became so cool.
   The mist rushed in my direction and said hello,
   My spirit lifted and I smiled.

   My thoughts further took me to a mountain spring, and my dog Sage appeared magically besides me.

   I sat down on a log of wood surrounded by a forest full of mystery, and my soul was at peace. My imagination… a vehicle transporting me to places I want to be. (April 14, 2018)

TRUTH & OTHER THINGS

1. When you are in the company of a wise person, listen with four ears.

2. Truth is a safe destination, enjoy the journey.

3. In life, we have to learn and, equally important, we have to unlearn.

4. Avoid self-pity like the plague.

5. I met the poor and the very poor, but the poorest of them all was the one incapable of love.

6. A person who always wants to display his knowledge has very little of it.

7. It is in your silences that you find words which matter.

8. A wise man gives advice to someone in the same way he would advise himself in a similar situation.

9. Truth comes with its own gravitas.

10. Truth is not much for fanfare.

11. Truth sings the longer song.

12. Truth doesn't need an orchestra.

13. Never delay love.

TRUTH & OTHER THINGS

14. Keep happy files in your mind's filling cabinet.

15. Do not take yourself too seriously. You are still very capable of slipping on a banana peel.

16. Her tongue was a shard of glass.

17. Unless you know yourself, you will not know anybody or anything.

18. The flatterer will never be the top guy.

19. When people say terrible things about others, most of the time, they are actually revealing what is in them.

20. The universe was there, when we arrived, it owes us nothing, but still gives us so much. There is something to learn from that.

21. Compassion, kindness and empathy are a part of intelligence.

22. If your life gave you a story to tell which can help others, you are doing ok.

THE TOXIC PERSON

1. They will bleed you dry, and then threaten to sue you for not having enough blood.

2. Some qualities of the toxic person:
    Blame, Complain, Mock, Compare, Keep taking, Love-less, to them Unity means only if you agree to everything they say, No real friends, gaslighting, no empathy, lying, disresectful, they make your happy space - dark, Demanding, Entitled, Authority without responsibility, attention seeking, Jealous, Rude, Putting others down, will try to put family and friends against you, extremely self-righteous.

    Hope you don't meet any of the above. But informed is empowered.

3. You are needed to love, to be kind, empathetic, helpful, strong, powerful, and wise to fight the hate, wickedness, avarice, covetousness and the vileness in this world and DEFEAT it.

OBSERVING PEOPLE

1. He wanted everyone to hear, so he said everything in stage whispers.

2. You are not supposed to know everything, so please stop behaving like you do.

3. He was the kind of person who could only love people posthumously.

FIND THE MAGIC

1. Believe in miracles, You are one!

2. Adversity muscles you up to learn and to overcome.

3. No biography is written about the complete pleasantness of life.

4. If life was always a bed of roses, half a thorn would kill you.

5. What you love to do, you will excel at.

6. To get mastery over anything, you will have to do those things over and over and over again.

7. Whenever you see a child, become one.

8. Follow your heart but don't lose your mind.

9. Have faith, can do.

10. Faith is the fuel of accomplishment.

11. If you think that you are right all the time, you are wrong.

12. Your mind knows, but your heart knows better, keep them aligned.

13. When the heart and mind are in agreement, there is every chance of success.

14. Work hard at working hard.

15. The measure of time and space was created for mankind by timeless and infinite God.

16. An intelligent man can turn complexity into simplicity

17. Be fascinated by what you don't know.

18. Keep the curiosity, keep the child in you alive, keep the wonder, learn.

TRUTH, MOTORCYCLES & MOTIVES

1. I will take your leave now, I have many things *not to do*.

2. Keep your ears open to hear the whisper of wisdom.

3. People think that their thoughts can't be seen, but you are what you think, so there you are.

4. If silence is better than what one has to say, let silence be.

5. Everything in a motor cycle is happy. Even the flat tyre.

6.
Feel the wind when you are riding your motorcycle. You will realise that it is alive.

7.
A person who lies to himself, will lie to everyone.

8.
A person who lies to himself, creates a person who doesn't exist.

9.
Truth throws the harder punch.

10. Being truthful to yourself is half the job done.

11. Motorcycles are pretty good therapists.

12. Motorcycles are a happy lot, ride safe.

13. If your motives are right, you sleep easy.

14. Pomposity is an attribute of the foolish.

15. If you are not fake, you don't have the headache of maintaing a false image.

16. While driving on rough terrain, I had to go over rocks, mud roads, hills, and a river. But the satisfaction of reaching my destination was much greater than if I had travelled by a smooth tarred road.

AS IT IS

1. The connection of generations is the building block of learning, growth and progress.

2. Some people practice foolishness so diligently that it starts to show on their faces.

3. Some people think that not smiling and wearing a frown is a religious activity.

4. There is so much to know and so much time, great, eternity is a long time.

5. Consciousness is an over-used word and many times used by the unconscious.

6. Divine revelation is a new consciousness.

7. When you get a promotion, look out for the person not clapping.

8. Hate sinks, love leaps.

9. Use your imagination, there is no limit put on it.

10. The only one to limit your imagination is you.

11. A good view can fire up your imagination.

12. Little things excite me like aaloo ka paratha and chai on a rainy day.

13. Make imagination your very good friend. It will make you grow and take you to new places, without cost.

OPINIONS, SCIENCE & THINGS

1. Comparison takes the magic out of things

2. Science cannot remain the same because greater truths will be discovered.

3. Men teach themselves to be blind to the truth - to wander the worlds that do not exist, lost.

4. Your are the only one with your DNA. You can be no other. You are special.

5. Don't say bad things about yourself to yourself.

6. Many times, man thinks why am I going through this? Why? But then thinks again.

7. Great answers have greater questions.

8. Paintings, quotes, poetry should not be explained too much.

9. To compare people all the time is a small mind activity.

10. To compare people vocally is to lose both of them.

11. People have opinions far from the truth. Those too they change every day.

12. Arrogance is air. To deflate is its destiny.

13. Forgiving people is a must to unburden yourself, but realising that a snake's nature is to bite, you no longer have to associate with them.

OPINIONS, SCIENCE & THINGS

14. While walking in the hills, the wind, mist and rain sang a beautiful song for me.

15. The terrible things he said about others is a vivid description of himself.

16. Without insight one walks on thin ice.

17. It is a pleasure to work with people who stick to the point and don't meander.

18. A revelation from the super natural, is a window to a new consciousness.

19. The pompous trip without the help of a banana peel.

20. Mistakes tell us what not to repeat. Wisdom tells us how not to.

21. Mankind will have to find the meaning of simplicity to be happy.

22. Don't fall for the line, "I am getting feelings for you again." It is a trap.

23. A humble man is an assured man.

24. He who thinks that others are inferior to him, learns from no one and so remains an "ignoramus."

MIND, MUSIC & KITES

1. Curbing your imagination is like not flying the kite higher.
   Believe me, it's more fun.

2. Let your soul touch the blue cloud and bring rain.

3. You must let your heart and mind talk to each other. Often.

4. When your heart and mind come to the same conclusion,
   You have a winner.

5. If you are bored with your self, you will be bored anywhere in the world.

6. The universe has its own music. Tune in.

7. The drop of water seemed to be clinging to the leaf, defying gravity.
   It did not want leave.

8. She wanted to kill the song in my heart, I just increased the volume. I
   hear she is humming it now.

9. Thinking about what could have been is a waste of time. Think about
   what can be now.

10. Some people are addicted to regret.

11. Do what you have to do with all your heart. Progress will be made.

MIND, MUSIC & KITES

12. Slow and steady progress makes things that last.

13. Being truthful to yourself is a big part of getting an education.

14. Disheveled hair sometimes hide a very sharp intellect.

15. Prayer is a two way process. Listen.

16. Somebody should write a good book about how to stop some people from talking, How to make someone shut up. I will buy it.

17. For some people, unity is that you agree to everything they say. They don't want unity, they want to dictate and control you.

18. When you first fall in love, everywhere you go, her perfume is there.

19. Good music can touch your soul and take you to magical places that you haven't been to before.

20. The kind of music you like to hear tells you something about yourself.

21. Some great tenors can be understood and move you even if they are singing in a language you don't know.

22. Listen to music most days and always sing in the bathroom.

23. Ghazals are the Indian blues.

24. A good song never ages.

25. Songs can bring back vivid memories.

MIND, MUSIC & KITES

26. Music and songs are a time machine.

27. For a celebration, nothing works like the dholak.

28. Help people cheerfully and quietly.

29. Give of yourself and increase.

30. Keep moving forward at whatever pace. If not your destination, you might see a new magical place.

31. To read is to travel beyond your boundaries and limitations.

32. A good book is timeless.

33. Don't judge people and things, understand them.

BUILD CHARACTER, BE JOYFUL

1. Be thankful and grateful every day. One thing to start you being thankful is that you are breathing.

2. Be thankful and appreciative. You will have a calm mind and good health.

3. Do good whenever you can. Anxiety will leave.

4. Think well of others. You will be happy.

5. Pray for someone who will never know. You will experience joy.

6. Help someone who can do nothing for you. You will build character.

7. Give advice thoughtfully, responsibly and correctly. Your conscience will be clear.

8. Teach what you know and you will be wiser.

9. Never stop learning. You will stay young.

10. Don't worry too much about what people think about you but keep an eagle's eye on your own thoughts. You will be better than you were. Every day.

11. Enjoy every walk you take. The elements will speak to you. The breeze will give you good news.

12. Arguing with a fool is a waste of your time not his.

13. What you learnt from your trials can be an education for many.

A GOOD WIND

1. Understand the difference between loneliness and solitude.

2. The One who created the universe loves you dearly. Never lose your confidence.

3. Be kind to the old. There is much we can learn from them. And we all will be old eventually. Hopefully.

6. Love creates a million rainbows.

7. Acts of kindness never go away. They travel with the wind and the breeze blows over the people who are hurting.

8. I was nothing and then I got lost, I roamed the wilderness for many years and then one day, a mysterious wind started to blow and lifting me up, Carried me to a Kingdom new but of ancient times. There I was found. Then I found myself.

9. Some things cannot be understood, they have to be experienced. That understanding becomes a part of you, increasing you.

MIRACLE OF THE UNIVERSE

1. The greatest truths are whispers in the universe scattered in the winds by the Creator. Some will hear.

2. Imagination can see more than your eye.

3. A good heart will hear things of great value.

4. More stars in the sky than grains of sand on earth. Stars exploding creating massive black holes. The worlds and the planets in an intriguing scientific motion, hanging on nothing.

The universe constantly expanding , infinite having no edge. Millions of magnetic fields creating a cosmic magic. The moon in the sky making tides in the seas of the earth. Moving billions of tons of water according to a divine will. Dark matter, dark energy a mystery.

A caterpillar transforms into a butterfly in the still of the night.

I sitting in a chair looking at a beautiful rose and a small forest in front of me.

I cannot be ordinary with all this around me. Neither can you.

5. Stop being lonely and begin to enjoy the solitude.

6. Times of solitude are required to discover yourself.

7. Be who you are. That's the only way to be.

8. Pray, because no man is an island.

THE FUTURE, THE YOUNG

1. Tell stories to your children and let them choose the ones they like.

2. Give books to your children and let them choose the ones they like.

3. Tell your children that they have great potential and they will excel at work that they enjoy doing.

4. Tell your children to work hard at working hard.

5. Teach your children the many meanings of love.

6. Teach your children the many meanings of compassion, kindness, politeness, empathy and fair play.

7. Encourage your children to play games outdoors.

8. Wisdom does not go after those who leave, if they repent and return, it accepts them with open arms.

9. If you fall but rise, you are now stronger than you were before the fall.

10. Thinking is a habit not seen in many people, while judging is rampant.

11. Do not try to make a poet, a doctor. You will kill his joy for life.

12. Teach your children that under no circumstances should a person treat another human being as inferior. Teach them that everybody is equal.

13. A kind word and a listening ear heals wounds.

14. Sometimes people don't need money, they need your time.
    Don't go away, stay awhile.

LIFE & SUCH THINGS

1. For evil and wickedness to lose, qualities and acts contrary to and opposing of them will have to garnered in a greater quantity. Then the active goodness in the multitude can push the evil to the edge and tip it over into the abyss. The goodness has to increase.

2. If there was no mystery, there would be no adventure.

3. If we knew everything, there would be no reason to get up in the morning.

4. Love people with a smiling heart.

5. The unreasonable shall not sleep, Reason will knock at night.

6. All great boxers are going to be philosophers.

7. Violence outside a boxing ring is an abomination and a horrific mistake.

8. In the rhythm of the universe, the Creator says, Love one another.

9. Sometimes people don't need money, they need your time. Don't go away, stay awhile.

10. He was judging everyone, until I told him that he did not have a degree in law and neither had the state appointed him judge. So what he was doing was illegal.

LIFE & SUCH THINGS

11. I looked for myself in people,
    but I did not find myself.
    I looked for myself in crowds, I wasn't there.
    I looked for myself in much merry-making,
    I was missing from there.

    One day, sitting alone, I caught a glimpse of myself.

    I got excited and started looking for Me in solitude.
    Slowly I started to appear to me as I am.

    The creator who gave the pulse to the earth, to live
    and thrive, also gave me a heart beat that makes
    me alive.
    I know that I am not alone.

    I am sufficient, I am enough.
    In Him , who is more than enough.

A FEW WORDS ON PARAMJIT SINGH

While reading the quotes, I experienced a pause, joy, laughter, an internal check about my own behaviours and a few epiphanies. Some of these stayed with me for days, and I used the insights in my work and other aspects of my life. This book will benefit people from any and every walk of life. It is blessed and the reader will be blessed too.

~ Payal Gupta, CEO, Celebratory Network

Paramjit Singh has been a source of profound wisdom and discernment for so many people. He listens with such compassion, and then gently guides us into making a decision that's balanced with loving care, whilst still upholding our faith and principles. His perspective has brought nuanced insight and clarity in complex situations. He somehow always manages to find meaning and uncover truths that resonate deeply, even amidst life's chaos. He constantly guide us with humility, care, and God-centered wisdom.

~ Tushar Gupta, Lead Product Manager,
   Packt Publishing, United Kingdom

From the author

मैंने सोचा मैं उसे माफ करूँगा तो वो ठीक होंगे	I thought if I forgive him he will get well.
उल्टा हुआ,	The reverse occured.
मैंने उसे माफ कयिा और मैं ठीक हुआ	I forgave him and I got well and whole.

If you can love, you can win!